STEVE NASH:
MOST VALUABLE PLAYER

PETER BAILEY

Fenn Publishing Company Ltd.
Bolton, Canada

Fenn Publishing Company Ltd.

STEVE NASH: MOST VALUABLE PLAYER

A Fenn Publishing Book / First Published in 2007

All rights reserved
Copyright 2007 © Moydart Press

Fenn Publishing Company Ltd.
Bolton, Ontario, Canada
www.hbfenn.com

The publisher gratefully acknowledges the support of the Canada Council for the Arts and the Ontario Arts Council for its publishing program.

We acknowledge the support of the Government of Ontario through the Ontario Media Development Corporation's Ontario Book Initiative.

 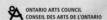

THE CANADA COUNCIL | LE CONSEIL DES ARTS
FOR THE ARTS | DU CANADA
SINCE 1957 | DEPUIS 1957

ONTARIO ARTS COUNCIL
CONSEIL DES ARTS DE L'ONTARIO

We acknowledge the financial support of the Government of Canada through the Book Publishing Industry Development Program (BPIDP) for our publishing activities.

Design: First Image
Printed and bound in Canada

Library and Archives Canada Cataloguing in Publication
Bailey, Peter, 1962-
Steve Nash : most valuable player / Peter Bailey.
ISBN 978-1-55168-319-5
1. Nash, Steve, 1974- --Juvenile literature.
2. Basketball players--Biography--Juvenile literature.
I. Title.
GV884.N37B35 2007   j796.323092   C2007-903069-6

CONTENTS

CHAPTER ONE

THE BOY FROM B.C.

"There was just a kind of a sparkle in his eyes that just tells you he's a little different than most guys."

High school coach Ian Hyde-Lay

Steve Nash was born a long, long way from Victoria, British Columbia, the small town in western Canada that he grew up in. Indeed, he was born in the capital city of South Africa, Johannesburg, and moved to Canada before he had celebrated his first birthday. Regardless of native land, Steve was athletic from the day he could walk, and for that he has his parents to thank.

Steve's father, John, was a professional soccer player in South Africa. He and his wife, Jean, were both born in England and moved to Johannesburg as a result of John's soccer career. In England, Jean was a superb netball player (a game similar to basketball), but they both wanted to move to Canada to raise a family. They moved first to Regina, Saskatchewan, then to Vancouver, and finally further west to Victoria on an island just across the Georgia Strait. By this time, Steve had two siblings, a brother, Martin, and a sister, Joann. They both also loved sports.

Martin went on to become a member of the Canadian national soccer team before embarking on a professional soccer career of his own, following in his father's footsteps. Joann also played soccer seriously and was captain of her team at the University of Victoria, where she played for three years.

Steve Nash was born a long, long way from Victoria, British Columbia.

Steve, meanwhile, excelled at many sports, including soccer where he was named team MVP in high school. This makes sense because his parents gave him a soccer ball as a present on his first birthday, and he started playing right away. In fact, the first word baby Steve apparently spoke was, "goal."

But he also loved lacrosse and baseball. He enjoyed basketball, yes, but his hero was Wayne Gretzky, the great hockey star of the Edmonton Oilers and later Los Angeles

Kings. Steve was inspired by the Great One's talent and dedication to the game he loved to play. What most people don't know about Steve was that even at a young age he was very successful at something else entirely—chess. Steve won three tournaments in chess during his early years at Mount Douglas High School. Perhaps it was this early understanding of how pieces moved on the chess board that helped make him one of the greatest passers in the history of the National Basketball Association (NBA).

It was in grade eight that Steve first played basketball, and he came home one day and told him mom that he was going to play in the NBA when he got older. "I didn't doubt him," she said. "Whether he'd make it or not, you don't know, but I knew he was going to give it a heck of a try because he works hard for what he gets."

> *He enjoyed basketball, yes, but his hero was Wayne Gretzky, the great hockey star of the Edmonton Oilers.*

However, like any kid, Steve found it difficult to balance school and sports, especially because he played so many sports and possessed a competitive personality. Steve enjoyed the physical challenges of trying his best against others, whether it was across the table studying a chess board, fighting for the ball on a soccer pitch, or trying to crack an opponent's defence on the hardwood floor in a basketball game.

As a direct result of his obsession with sports, Steve's school grades declined. While his parents wanted Steve to maintain a physically healthy and active lifestyle, they also wanted him to receive an excellent education. At the age of 16, Steve missed dozens of classes during the first three months of the 1990-91 school year, sometimes because of sports and sometimes because he simply didn't want to go. He preferred playing basketball in the gym. During the start of the school year, Steve helped the Mount Douglas team win the AAA provincial soccer

Steve comes from a soccer-playing family and still loves the game both as a player and a fan.

Steve not only enjoys the big show of the NBA but also sharing what he knows with kids who haven't had the same opportunities he's had.

championship—and he was named MVP of the tournament! That wasn't good enough for his parents.

So, they withdrew their eldest son from Mount Douglas and enrolled him at St. Michael's University School, a private school, in Victoria. This was at the start of December 1990, but because the transfer occurred during the school year it meant Steve had to miss an entire year of basketball. This was due to something called transfer rules, and these rules were in place to make sure a player didn't play for two teams in any one season.

This transfer was an important event for two reasons. One, Steve began to take basketball more seriously than any other sport by this time, so missing a year was a really big deal. And, two, if Steve wanted to earn a basketball scholarship to a university in the United States, which is how most players get to the NBA, he was sacrificing a year at a critical time of his life.

it was clear he was a special player, especially in his ability to pass the ball as opposed to shooting it.

Steve began playing basketball in 1987 while attended Hillcrest Elementary School, the place he attended before Arbutus Junior Secondary and then Mount Douglas. Yet right away, it was clear he was a special player, especially in his ability to pass the ball as opposed to shooting it. He also took the game really seriously, not just during games but also away from the cheering crowds. This was when Steve first started to practice every aspect of the game, from lay-ups to free throws and three-point shots to jump shots from every area of the floor. And then there was the dribbling, bouncing a ball every free moment, working on his coordination and learning to make the ball an extension of his arms.

Once he got to St. Michael's, he made up for not being on the team by practicing his every waking hour. He would dribble a ball to school, using first the right hand, then the left hand, to ensure that he became ambidextrous, an essential skill in the NBA. He stayed after school and practiced his shooting, and took hundreds of free throws to master the art of that shot. In a strange way, his not being allowed to play might actually have made him a better player because he focused so hard on practicing. By the time he was allowed to play for the team again, his skills had developed so much more completely.

"I just loved basketball so much and played so much and worked so hard—to be punished for transferring schools...it was a difficult year. But it was something I had to do," he said with typical determination many years later. "I wouldn't be where I am today if I hadn't made that move. It's that simple."

> "I wouldn't be where I am today if I hadn't made that move."

Steve's reputation in the school system was so strong that when he made the switch from Mount Douglas to St. Michael's even the local newspapers wrote about it. Here was a star 16-year-old player, in Grade 11, moving to a school to focus on academics. Just a season ago, Steve was named the tournament MVP in the 1990 B.C. Junior Secondary School championship tournament, playing for the Arbutus Aztecs. The team lost the championship finals to Spencer Middle School, but Steve made a great impression on everyone who watched.

That summer, he played for the B.C. under-17 all-star team where he was the best point guard in the tournament. He also played for the national junior team those months and in fact played so well in his one game that he was the last cut prior to the world championships, a heart-breaking event but one that made him stronger. Still, many of his teammates from Arbutus went on to join him at Mount Douglas for Grade 11.

Steve's transfer to St. Michael's wasn't all bad. Mount Douglas had had a new coach to start this season, and he didn't encourage Steve to the extent Steve had hoped. Steve agreed with his parents that maybe a fresh start would be the best thing, and he was further encouraged when he met the new team's basketball coach, Ian Hyde-Lay, who was very supportive of Steve's skills and ambitions.

"Steve came into our school...and immediately became the leader," Ian said. "The tougher the situation, the more he wanted to be right in there taking the last shot or whatever. There was just something about him. There was just kind of a sparkle in his eyes that just tells you he's a little different than most guys."

Everything was set, and Steve started classes at St. Michael's in early December. The one thing he had not been able to prepare for was just how difficult it was to practice all the time and then sit at the end of the bench when the Blue Devils played a game. Steve was frustrated beyond words by having to sit out for the year, but he wanted to be with his new teammates all the same. All the while, though, he was being tutored by his coach. Ian would even play Steve one-on-one, showing him the tricks of the trade, teaching him the fundamentals, and impressing on Steve how important a simple game plan was to success. Don't try to be fancy when you can be simple, he would say. Don't try to drive to the net when you can stop quickly and take an easy jump shot. Don't fancy dribble to impress. Fancy moves might look good, but simple moves win games, he said over and over again.

> "Steve came into our school... and immediately became the leader."

It's a rare thrill for a Canadian to be featured on a Wheaties box of cereal.
Only Wayne Gretzky and Mario Lemieux appeared before Steve.

Steve Nash: Most Valuable Player

Steve received some very good news early in 1991 when he was invited by the Canadian national team coach, Ken Shields, to practice during a week and a half long training camp at the University of Victoria. The 17-year-old Steve would get a great chance to gauge his abilities against the best senior players in the country. Coach Shields asked Steve to play point guard, and although Steve was shorter, weighed less, and was physically smaller than everyone else at the camp, he looked pretty good in scrimmages. More impressive, he wasn't scared or intimidated, even though most of the players played in the NBA or leagues in Europe.

By the fall of 1991, Steve was entering Grade 12 and was about to begin one of the most important years of his life. It was his final year of high school, but although he hoped to earn a scholarship to an American university, he had missed a year of playing and had not been scouted by anyone. That's right—not one scout had seen him play. Steve knew he had to play well right away if he hoped to "attract attention," as they say.

> He was a Canadian playing an American game, in a small city in British Columbia.

He did and he didn't. That is, he did play well, but he didn't attract attention. There was another problem that prevented him from being scouted. He was a Canadian playing an American game, in a small city in British Columbia. He wasn't tall. He wasn't flashy. He didn't play like Michael Jordan. He was a point guard, a very demanding position on court that only few players have the talent to fill. Canada didn't have a pro basketball team at this time, and scouts simply never came north to look for new talent. In the whole history of the NBA, maybe five or six players had been Canadian.

"It was frustrating," Steve admitted later, "because I was watching college basketball on TV all the time thinking that I could play with this guy and that guy, that I could play at certain schools, and no one would ever show any interest."

That's where his coach came into the picture. Ian sent out letters to just about every American university that had a decent basketball program. He told each school that Steve was a tremendous talent and that they should take the time to watch him play. The silence was deafening. The rejection letters accumulated. By Christmas, Steve had his St. Michael's team in first place and was playing sensationally well, but not one scout had paid him a visit. Not one.

Santa Clara was no powerhouse basketball program.

At about the same time, in December 1991, during his Grade 12 year, coach Hyde-Lay and Ken Shields extended an invitation to Steve that made a lasting impression. They took him to Seattle to watch an NBA game featuring the Super Sonics and Golden State. They even got seats right behind the Warriors' bench. Steve not only got a sense of the speed and skill of the game, he also saw what amazing condition the players were in. They had bodies that were the result of years of training and hard work.

Then, Steve had a bit of luck. Two men from a small place called Santa Clara University in California asked to see a tape of Steve play. Ian immediately gave them a tape. Dick Davey and Scott Gradin were impressed and kept enquiring about him. On the one hand, Steve was glad to have earned some attention, somewhere. On the other hand, Santa Clara was no powerhouse basketball program. Still, it was better to be wanted by someone than no one. Meanwhile, Steve continued to take his team to win after win during the season. In all, the Blue Devils had a 50-4 record on the year, and three of those four losses came when Steve was out of the lineup with a slightly separated shoulder.

The year ended with the Blue Devils playing in the prestigious B.C. Senior AAA Boys Basketball Championship, the most important tournament for this age group. Steve was playing his best, and Dick Davey decided to travel to British Columbia to watch him in person. Dick stayed for two games. He met Steve and his family and extended an invitation for Steve to play at Santa Clara on full scholarship in the fall. He was that sure of Steve's abilities. Dick returned home, and Steve continued to take his team through the tournament to the finals. In his last game of high school basketball, Steve scored 31 points and led his team to a lop-sided 76-48 win over the Pitt Meadows Marauders, the largest margin of victory in the tournament's history. Steve was named tournament MVP.

> *Steve was on a plane heading to Santa Clara for two days.*

Just a few days later, Steve was on a plane heading to Santa Clara for two days. He was going to meet the coaching staff, the players on the current team, and see the university and city. Steve was impressed with everything he saw during his brief visit. He and the coaches got along well, and when he scrimmaged with the players he realized right away he was in a superior league to what he was used to. Maybe he had wanted to go to a more famous university, but Steve was happy to play with any Division I team in the NCAA. A few weeks later, he committed to playing for Santa Clara for the upcoming 1992-93 season.

CHAPTER TWO

ON THE ROAD TO SANTA CLARA

The first "wow" moment of Steve's life occurred on December 11, 1995, when *Sports Illustrated* featured Steve in its magazine.

Santa Clara was not a big university and it was located in a small town that gave Steve the feeling of being in Victoria. That was where the similarities ended. Steve arrived on campus in late August full of hope and energy, but slowly these were taken from him during his first weeks with the basketball team, the Broncos. Steve was more homesick than he had imagined. All of the familiar things that had been part of his life for so many years simply weren't there. His family, his friends, the school gym—all were gone.

And while Steve had always had plenty of confidence in his ability to play basketball at a high level, even that started to disappear. He was now playing Division I ball, and he found the players were much bigger, much stronger and more physical, and much more skilled than he had expected. In short, Steve had a really tough time adjusting.

To make matters worse, his coach, Dick Davey, the same man who had recruited him for Santa Clara, was really tough on him in practice. Steve's trademark passing was lacking its accuracy and effectiveness. His speed seemed wanting, and even his enthusiasm seemed to be ineffective against his teammates.

> *All of the familiar things that had been part of his life for so many years simply weren't there.*

But assistant coach Scott Gradin was supportive when coach Davey was tough, and Steve simply refused to be beaten by a bad attitude. He kept pushing and trying. He dribbled a tennis ball all around campus to improve his hand-eye coordination and his hand skills. Just like at home, he also practiced early in the morning and late at night in the gym, working on all aspects of the game. And, in truth, the more his coach and teammates got mad at him and pushed him to do better, the tougher Steve got mentally and the better it was for him in the long run.

As the college basketball season began, Steve was clearly the second-best point guard on the team. The best was John Woolery, who regularly made Steve look bad in practice. As a result, Steve started the year sitting on the bench, meaning he would come into a game only for a few minutes to give John a rest. Steve was a substitute, and in the early going he played like one. When he got a chance to play, he was nervous. His shooting was poor, and he made several turnovers because of poor passes and weak dribbling.

But a month into the season, John hurt his knee and missed three games. Coach Davey decided to give Steve all of John's playing time, and Steve was determined to take advantage of this opportunity. He did.

> *Steve was a substitute, and in the early going he played like one.*

In his first-ever start as a college basketball player, against Minnesota, Steve turned in a star performance. He led the team in scoring, was outstanding in three-point shooting, and, most important, did not commit a single turnover the whole game. He was almost as dominating in the next two games. As a result, coach Davey had to find a way to give Steve more playing time when John returned to the lineup. Steve played shooting guard, and given the opportunity to play most of every game, he excelled.

Yet, it seemed as though the better he played in games, the tougher the coach was with him in practice. This hardly seemed fair, but Steve understood the nature of his relationship with the coach. Steve had been a huge fan of Wayne Gretzky growing up, yet even the greatest hockey player of all time was not praised by his coach all the time. No. Glen Sather, coach of the Edmonton Oilers, always pushed the Great One and his teammates—Mark Messier, Paul Coffey, Glenn Anderson—to do more and more and more. A good coach will push a player to improve beyond what

Steve shows the art of the "fade-away jumper," a jump shot made while falling away from the net to avoid being blocked.

Steve avoids the defence to made a left-handed lay-up, one of the hardest shots in basketball for a natural right-handed shooter to make.

the player thought he could do. And guess what? A good player always managed to exceed even the coach's high expectations.

So it was with Steve. The coach may have been hard on him, but Steve responded by becoming better and better all the time. As his freshman (first year) season was coming to an end, Steve took the Broncos on a long winning streak that pushed the team into the West Coast Conference tournament. The Broncos advanced to the finals of this event, and this was a huge accomplishment because the winner advanced to the NCAA finals which was called "March Madness." This was the most important basketball event in the United States outside of the NBA. It featured the top 64 teams in the country playing an elimination series of games to determine the best basketball team. Unfortunately, Santa Clara would have to beat top-ranked Pepperdine to get there.

The date was March 8, 1993. Pepperdine jumped into an early lead and by halftime they were in full control. However, Steve came out in the second half and played, quite simply, the best basketball of his life. He scored the first eight points to start the half and hit one three-pointer after another. By the time the final buzzer sounded, the Broncos had defeated the Pepperdine Waves, 73-63. Steve had an incredible 23 points, one-third his team's entire total! He was named MVP of the tournament, the first time ever a first-year player had been so honoured. In just one game, he had become a hero at Santa Clara.

> *The coach may have been hard on him, but Steve responded by becoming better and better all the time.*

It was now time for "March Madness." The tournament was divided into four sections of 16 teams each, and the Santa Clara Broncos were ranked 15th. Their first opponent was Arizona, ranked number two, in a game set for Salt Lake City, Utah. It seemed as though there was little hope for Santa Clara.

No one makes behind-the-back passes with the trickery and accuracy of Steve.

Steve Nash: Most Valuable Player

But again, Steve rallied the team to a most incredible victory with his play in the dying minutes. The Broncos were fighting to the end, and with less than a minute to go they were within a point of victory. Arizona repeatedly fouled Steve in order to send him to the free-throw line. They assumed he would miss and then they would get control of the ball themselves. The arena was packed with 12,000 screaming fans. The pressure was intense, but Steve nailed six straight free throws and the Broncos won, 64-61. It was a victory made possible only because of the endless hours Steve spent practicing free throws in the gym at Mount Douglas and St. Michael's in Victoria. That's what he thought about as he made those clutch shots in the most important NCAA tournament.

Steve's second year at Santa Clara, 1993-94, was simply bigger and better than year one, another sign of his ability to improve constantly. As a result of his great finish to his first season, Steve now was a regular starter as a shooting guard. He still was not ready to fill John Woolery's shoes as a point guard because John was still more experienced, but that didn't matter. Steve was playing every game. As a sophomore, he averaged nearly 15 points a game, and the year after he took another significant step to making it to the NBA. For 1994-95, he stepped in as point guard after John graduated, and now Steve was playing the position he felt most comfortable in. He led all West Coast teams with a 20.9 points per game average and a 6.4 assists per game average. As a result, he was named his conference's most valuable player.

The pressure was intense, but Steve nailed six straight free throws and the Broncos won.

This paved the way for his senior year, his final year of university basketball, the year when he would either play himself into the NBA or take himself far, far away from it. This was the year the pro scouts started watching all top prospects carefully, trying to figure out who to draft and who to ignore. For Santa

Clara, the first big date of the 1995-96 season was the Maui Invitational tournament in November. The small team from Santa Clara played the UCLA Bruins, the prior year's national champions and always one of the best teams in the country.

Once again, however, Steve played better than anyone expected. He scored 19 points and added seven assists against the Bruins, and the Broncos shocked the top nation with a resounding 78-69 victory. The Broncos lost their next game but in game three they again beat a supposedly superior opponent, this time downing Michigan State, 77-71. While at the tournament, Steve got to meet the greatest passer in the history of basketball, Earvin "Magic" Johnson. "Magic" gave Steve an autographed picture and signed it "From Big Magic to Little Magic," in honour of Steve's amazing passing ability.

> *Much of his senior year was a test unlike he had experienced before.*

The first "wow" moment of Steve's life occurred on December 11, 1995, when *Sports Illustrated* featured him in its magazine. That was when the rest of the basketball world really learned about Steve's life, his ambition, and, most of all, his skill.

Much of his senior year was a test unlike he had experienced before, though. For all of his life, Steve was the underdog, the guy no one expected to do well yet somehow did. But by his senior year, he was the star of Santa Clara and opponents keyed on him as the most important player on the team. "Stop Nash and you beat the Broncos," was how other teams started to plan their games against Santa Clara.

As a result, Steve didn't have the same impressive statistics as he had the year before, but he became an even better player. He learned how to get open when he was double-teamed. He learned how to make passes when opponents played him to shoot. He learned how to inspire his teammates to rise to the challenge. By year's end, he was once again named conference MVP, a rare accomplishment in NCAA Division I history.

It was now time for "March Madness," 1996 edition. Santa Clara played University of Maryland Terrapins, and despite being hobbled by a leg injury Steve led the way to victory by scoring 28 points and adding 12 assists, one of the best games of his life. Although the Broncos lost their next game to Kansas, Steve had played well enough in his final year to rank as one of the greatest young players in the world. He finished his career with Santa Clara as the all-time leader in assists, three-point shooting, and free-throw percentage.

There was only one more test for Steve, and that was a training camp at the end of the year for all of the nation's top prospects. It gave the players a chance to play against the best, and it gave scouts a chance to evaluate players under tough circumstances. Despite having a leg injury, Steve was among the best players at the camp and was named to the all-star team for the event. Once again, he had proved himself.

Steve graduated from Santa Clara with a degree in sociology, but he hoped never to have to use that degree. He was counting on everything going right on June 26, 1996, at the Continental Airlines Arena in New Jersey, home rink of the NHL's Devils. It was draft day in the NBA, and Steve was there with his family and agent to see what team he would be playing with and where on the list he would be drafted. It was, in fact, the most talented pool of drafted players in NBA history.

Kobe Bryant was drafted by Charlotte, only to be traded to the Los Angeles Lakers. Allen Iverson was selected by Philadelphia first overall, and the Toronto Raptors took Marcus Camby. Stephon Marbury went to Milwaukee and Minnesota grabbed Ray Allen. And with the 15th pick overall, the Phoenix Suns chose 6'3" 195-pound point guard from Santa Clara—Steve Nash!

CHAPTER THREE

THE NBA

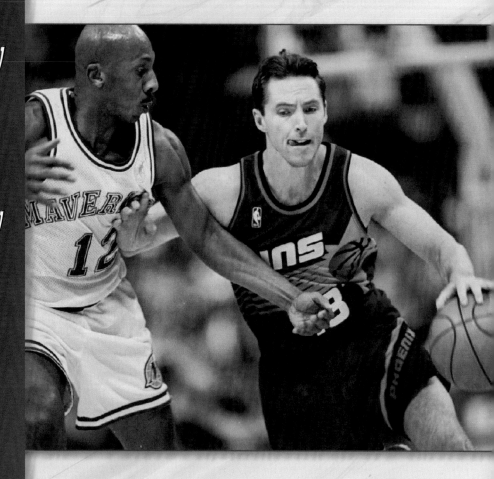

"I'm going to be a really good player and I'm going to help the team a lot."

Steve, after being drafted by Phoenix

S Steve became the highest-drafted Canadian in NBA history (Bill Wennington was 16th overall back in 1985). In fact, he was only the third Canadian picked since 1989! His home and native land had produced thousands of professional hockey players over the years, but Steve was breaking new ground on the hard court for Canada.

"The NBA is the dream of my life," he said after being drafted. "I know a lot of people may not know my name all that well, but I'm excited for the opportunity to prove myself at this level."

Although he was happy to be with Phoenix, not everyone in Phoenix was happy to be with him. Many fans had booed his selection because they wanted the Suns to choose another player, but Steve took it all in stride. "I don't look like I'm going to be a tremendous basketball player on appearance," he said, humbly. "I probably would've booed myself too, but I'm going to be a really good player and I'm going to help the team a lot. I have a lot of faith in myself, and hopefully they'll enjoy watching me play.... I'm excited to be in a passionate city."

> *"I know a lot of people may not know my name all that well, but I'm excited for the opportunity to prove myself at this level."*

It was with joy and a bit of fear that Steve reported to his first professional training camp. He was happy to be pursuing his dream, but in Phoenix there were not one but two other point guards who were more experienced and, quite simply, better than him—Kevin Johnson and Sam Cassell.

Kevin Johnson was nearing the end of a great career. He started back in 1987 with Cleveland but was now in his tenth season with Phoenix. He was among the top scorers in the league still and averaged nearly ten assists a game throughout his career. This was a superb record. Sam Cassell was a two-time NBA champion with the Houston Rockets and one of the best in the game. He could pass, shoot, and play with intensity. That's just the role Steve wanted to play, but he was going to have to be patient and wait for his chances to prove himself.

So, yes, Steve was happy, but he also knew most of his NBA time in his first year would come in practice, not in games. He knew he would be on the bench most of the time. He knew the pressure he would be under to perform well during those precious few shifts he might get when he would be asked to come on so that the stars, Kevin and Jason, could take a breather.

> *He also realized that he could learn from two of the best point guards in the league.*

Steve was always positive and confident, though. He also realized that he could learn from two of the best point guards in the league. He was determined to practice as hard as ever, and watch them and learn from them. Steve was, after all, only 22 years old with no NBA experience. More important, he had to learn all the things about playing in the NBA apart from actually passing and shooting. For instance, because Phoenix was a team on the west coast, he would be doing way more traveling than he ever experienced before. He was also going to have to play 82 regular season games, as well as exhibition and playoff games. That's a lot more than he ever played at Santa Clara or in B.C.

As a first-round draft choice, he also had the pressure of dealing with the media and the fans. Every day, after every game or practice, there would be large groups of media, and Steve would have to be prepared to answer questions about his performance. In truth, it might have been a blessing in disguise that he didn't become the starting point guard right away—it might have been too much too handle with everything else going on, too.

Steve knocks the ball away from L.A. Lakers guard Derek Fisher, using speed and unexpected hand quickness.

As it turned out, Steve played quite a bit during training camp because Kevin Johnson was injured. Of course, he had adjustments to make, just as he had when he transferred to St. Michael's and just as he had when he first joined Santa Clara. Regardless what sport an athlete played, the biggest adjustment about moving up a level is the speed of the game. Basketball was no different. If Steve had one second to make a play at the university level, he had only half a second in the NBA. Although he earned a reputation as a great passer and long-range shooter, Steve would also have to work on his defence if he were to make it in the NBA. If other teams found he was weak defensively, they'd simply attack him at every opportunity and draw fouls or make an easy basket.

> *Steve scored 17 points and contributed 12 assists, playing nearly every minute of the game.*

All of this took Steve weeks to get used to, and so when he got into his first game, he knew it would be for just a few minutes. That game took place on November 1, 1996, in Los Angeles, against Shaquille O'Neal and the Lakers. There were two other moments that defined his rookie season. The first came two weeks later when the Suns travelled to Steve's native Vancouver to play the Grizzlies, one of two new NBA expansion franchises located in Canada. It was obviously a huge game for Steve because he was returning home, but Kevin Johnson and Sam Cassels were still going to get most of the playing time.

Fate stepped in on the way to the game, though. Kevin suffered an injury and was still not able to play, and then Sam got sick and was also unable to play. That left Steve in the starter's role at point guard, and he responded in superstar fashion. Steve scored 17 points and contributed 12 assists, playing nearly every minute of the game. The Suns lost, but he was hailed a hero by his family and fans in British Columbia who remembered him for all his years as a kid with big ambitions.

Steve commits a foul against Atlanta's Dikembe Mutombo
but prevents an easy basket in the process.

Steve puts the finishing touches on a perfectly executed lay-up.

Steve gives Michele Timms a hug during the 1998 All-Star Game celebrations. Timms is a star with Phoenix of the Women's NBA, and the two competed in a "2Ball" event, featuring an NBA and WNBA player.

The second important event of the year wasn't such good news for Steve. The team traded Sam in a big deal which saw the Suns acquire Jason Kidd. Jason was like another Steve, only a bit more established. Jason was a point guard, in his third year. In 1994, as a rookie, he stepped right in and played almost every minute of every game for the Dallas Mavericks. He was that good. Now, instead of playing behind two veteran, sensational point guards, Steve was playing behind one older guard and one who was going to be in the league another ten or 12 years.

By the end of his rookie season, Steve had hardly realized his dreams. Yes, he was in the NBA, but he played an average of just ten minutes a game and contributed 3.3 points a game. In the playoffs, he played even less. These were not impressive numbers. Even still, Steve went into his second season with a positive attitude, hoping to continue to learn so that when he got the chance to play, he would do extremely well.

The team traded Sam in a big deal which saw the Suns acquire Jason Kidd.

Indeed, Steve played a lot more in 1997-98, and he played well. More than any other player on the team, the point guard is the on-court leader. He is the player who takes the ball up court. He is the one to call the plays, see what the defence is doing, make the initial play to generate a scoring chance. Even in just his second season, it was clear Steve was able to do this well. He was now playing almost half a game each night, and he was averaging about nine points and three assists a game, pretty good numbers for half a game.

When a player is drafted into the NBA, he signs a two-year contract which pays him a low salary by NBA standards (although it is a very very good salary by most people's standards!). So, after Steve's second year, his contract expired and both he and

Steve bravely stands his ground as New York Knicks' guard Jamal Crawford commits an offensive foul to give Steve's team the ball.

Steve drives hard to the net and makes a lay-up, driving past the Dallas Mavericks defence which doesn't want to foul him.

Phoenix had to make a decision about what to do next. Kevin Johnson was not going to be around much longer, but Jason Kidd certainly was still the star of the team. The Suns could only offer Steve a contract much less than Jason because Steve was, sort of, the backup who was almost as good as the starter but who had to be paid like the backup. In short, he needed a new team, and the Suns realized this.

> All that was left now was for him to go out on the court and do what he knew he could do—dominate.

At the 1998 draft, held in Vancouver, Phoenix traded Steve to the Dallas Mavericks, a team that had missed the playoffs for the last eight years. It was a team that had many young players, though, a team that was ready to make a move in the NBA. And Steve was now a part of this. The Mavericks even gave him a six-year contract as soon as they traded for him, giving Steve the comfort of knowing he was going to be important to the team for a long time.

Steve now had two years of NBA play under his belt. He had a long-term contract and a team that wanted him. All that was left now was for him to go out on the court and do what he knew he could do—dominate.

Steve shows his perfect passing form during the skills competition of the 2005 All-Star festivities.

CHAPTER FOUR

DALLAS GIVES STEVE A CHANCE TO SHINE

"There are a lot of great players in this league, but to be put in the upper group was always something I expected of myself."

Steve Nash

T The trade from Phoenix to Dallas involved several players. The Mavericks acquired Steve in exchange for four players—Bubba Wells, Martin Muursepp, Pat Garrity, and a first-round draft choice in 1999 (Shawn Marion). This alone showed how much Dallas admired Steve's talents.

Miracles don't happen overnight, though. Yes, Steve was entering his third year in the NBA, but it was still his first with a new team and his first where he'd be playing regularly. That meant another move up, another series of adjustments, another period of getting better and taking his game to a higher level.

The 1998-99 season was fraught with bad news for Steve. First, the season was delayed for many weeks because the players and the league could not agree on a new contract. In the end, the season consisted of just 50 regular-season games instead of the usual 82, and this meant that every team would have to play better faster if it hoped to make the playoffs. This meant more pressure on Steve.

> *Steve suffered from something known as spondylolisthesis, a fancy way of saying a bad back.*

Then, Steve experienced injury trouble. Most of the time it was a nagging foot injury or a painful cut on his shooting hand, but he played through it all. The one exception was a back injury. Steve suffered from something known as spondylolisthesis, a fancy way of saying a bad back. That's why when he took a break and went to the sidelines, he didn't sit in a chair like the other players. No. Instead, he lay down on the floor, where he could stretch his back and relieve it of all pressure. This condition caused him to miss ten games, 20 per cent of the season, and caused him discomfort for many other games.

Worse of all, the home fans in Dallas started to boo Steve. They realized how many players the team had traded to get him,

Steve will not be denied the basket, even though Houston forward Keny Thomas does his best to stop him.

realized that the team counted on him to take it to the playoffs after eight years of misery. Yet here he was, late in the season, averaging less than ten points a game and playing on a team that was going to miss the playoffs yet again.

The best thing that came out of this 1998-99 season, in fact, was his friendship with teammate Dirk Nowitzki. Dirk was only 20 years old and came to the NBA from Germany. He was seven feet tall, a giant even among NBA players, and was also important to the team's success. The two became close friends and lived near each other, so they frequently went to practices and games together. They supported each other through tough times—the fans expected a lot from Dirk as well—and knew they could team up on court to be an effective pairing.

After a busy summer with the Canadian national team, Steve arrived at training camp for the 1999-2000 season feeling exhausted from his non-stop schedule but also energized by helping Canada qualify for the 2000 Olympics (which he expected to play in as well). The result was an improvement in his own play, but the Mavericks had done little during the off season to build a winning team. He and Dirk got better and became even closer friends, but the biggest difference with the team happened off court.

Mark immediately improved the Mavericks in ways the players appreciated.

During the season, Mark Cuban bought the team. He had made an enormous amount of money in developing internet sites, but he loved basketball and wanted to own a team.

Mark immediately improved the Mavericks in ways the players appreciated. He bought a private plane for the team to use for travel to road games. He upgraded the dressing room and made it clear that he was willing to do everything possible to give the players an environment in which they could be comfortable. In return, of course, he expected the team to win, and this put pressure on Steve again. The Mavericks barely missed the playoffs that year, but in 2000-01, they made it easily.

Over the two years, the team improved from a record of 40-42 to 53-29. Steve virtually doubled his statistics, averaging more than 15 points and seven assists a game in 2000-01. And Dirk also had a breakout season, averaging nearly 22 points and more than nine rebounds a game. The better these two friends played, the better were the chances of the Mavericks winning. The team also had a third superstar in the making, Michael Finley. Michael and Steve played together in Phoenix for a short time, and now they were both star players in Dallas.

Dallas ended up losing in the next round to San Antonio, but the mood in the dressing room afterward was one of optimism.

Now that the team was in the playoffs for the first time since 1990, it had to play the mighty Utah Jazz in the first round. The Jazz won the first two games of the best-of-five pretty easily, and this put Dallas in the worst position possible. One more loss and their season would be over.

Not so fast. Steve helped the team win game three, and in game four he scored 27 points in a huge win to send the series back to Utah for the deciding game. Utah was in the lead for almost the entire game, but then in the fourth quarter, Steve put it all on the line. He nailed three pointers, played hard on defence, and ignited a stunning rally that saw Dallas win by a single point, 84-83. Steve called this the best game of his career to date outside the Olympics.

Dallas ended up losing in the next round to San Antonio, but the mood in the dressing room afterward was one of optimism. Steve couldn't wait for the next year to begin. Sure enough, there were more improvements in 2001-02. Steve, Dirk,

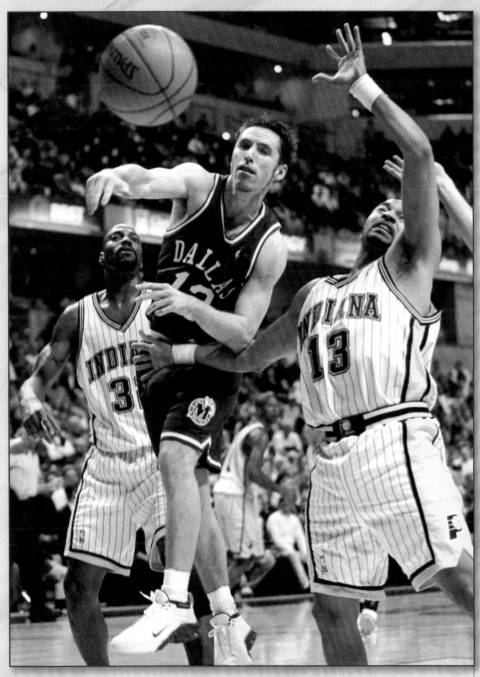

Despite being trapped by Mark Jackson of the Indiana Pacers (#13),
Steve dishes the ball off to an open man for the easy shot.

Minnesota's Wally Szczerbiak may be much taller, but Steve knows if he keeps going he'll either reach the net or draw a foul.

and Michael continued to lead the way, and the Mavericks improved their record to 57-25 on the year. At mid-season, Steve played in his first All-Star Game. It was the kind of honour that showed that everyone around the league now considered him one of the best players in the game. Steve was happy, but not surprised by the way his career was taking off.

"There are a lot of great players in this league, but to be put in the upper group was always something I expected of myself," Steve admitted. "Whether I get there and stay there is another thing, but it's something I believe I can do."

It was around this time that Steve used his fame for off-court contributions. He created the Steve Nash Foundation, a charitable organization which helps kids less fortunate. It also demonstrated that although he was great at making assists in the NBA, he was just as great at assisting people in the real world where life is so much more important than basketball.

> Steve was happy, but not surprised by the way his career was taking off.

The 2002 All-Star Game was near and dear to Steve's heart for another reason. The team's final game before the All-Star Game break took place in New Jersey, and that night his teammates took him out in nearby New York City to celebrate his 28th birthday. Steve took a liking to the group's waitress, a woman named Alejandra Amarilla. She came to New York from Paraguay, and the two started a conversation that continued to this day. They spent most of that summer together, and when the next basketball season started she moved to Dallas to be with him. A little while later, they were married and started a family!

Not surprisingly, the 2002-03 season was Steve's best so far. He was now comfortable in Dallas and had a great friend as a teammate. He was in love. He was in the prime of his life physically. He was ready to do something special. The Mavericks started the year with a perfect 14-0 record and continued their torrid pace all year. The Steve Nash-Dirk Nowitzki combination was now the best in the league, and the two combined for an average of nearly 40 points a game. At one point, Steve set a team record by making 49 straight free throws. Both Steve and Dirk were named to play in the All-Star Game, in Atlanta, but they were disappointed when Michael Finley was left off the team. By the end of the year, Dallas had a record of 60-22, another team record, and they were now one of the favourites at the start of the playoffs.

> *The Trail Blazers roared back to tie the series, and Steve had perhaps his worst games of the year.*

Dallas's first-round opponent was Portland, and it looked like no contest when the Mavericks won the first three games of the best-of-seven. But the Trail Blazers roared back to tie the series, and Steve had perhaps his worst games of the year. In game seven, though, he and Dirk were unstoppable, scoring 52 of the team's points in a convincing 107-95 win.

Next up were the Sacramento Kings, and this turned out to be a more even and dramatic series. The Kings won the first game, but Dallas came back to win the next two. Sacramento won game four, and then Dallas and the Kings won the next pair of games. This set up another game seven showdown, in Dallas. Steve anchored the team from the back, scoring 18 points and leading the Mavs to a 112-99 win to advance to the conference finals against the San Antonio Spurs.

San Antonio was a tough team, though. It had Tim Duncan, a giant of a man with a soft touch around the net, as well as Tony Parker and Manu Ginobili. Steve and Dirk combined for an incredible 60 points in game one to lead Dallas to a 113-100 win in the series opener, but that was the best fans would see from Dallas this series.

Steve Nash: Most Valuable Player

Atlanta's Alan Henderson (#42) and Jason Terry (#31) can only watch as
Steve flies through the air for a shot.

Los Angeles Lakers' giant Shaquille O'Neal leaves Steve no choice but to make a pass on this play!

The Spurs won game two, and in game three Dirk suffered a knee injury that sidelined him for the rest of the year. The Spurs won that game and the next to take a commanding 3-1 lead in the series. Although Steve mustered the resolve to win game five by a 103-91 score, it was all San Antonio in game six and the Spurs advanced to the championship finals while the Mavericks went home. Nevertheless, it was a great season for the team and something to build on.

The Mavericks failed to do that, however. The 2003-04 season was one of change and disappointment as owner Mark Cuban brought in several new players and upset the team chemistry. Steve had a good year, but now as one of the team's veterans the players looked to him for leadership. Although the Mavericks finished with a terrific 52-30 record, they lost in the first round of the playoffs to Sacramento in seven games. Steve played really well that series, but the Kings had also made it a priority to guard him closely because they knew if they could limit his greatness, they could win. They did.

> *So much was expected of him, yet his contract was set to expire at the end of the season.*

For Steve, it was a strange year. So much was expected of him, yet his contract was set to expire at the end of the season and Mark Cuban hadn't really indicated he wanted Steve back with the team. After the early elimination from the playoffs, Steve didn't know what to think. His loyalty was to Dallas, but he didn't feel the same was true the other way. Mark made a contract offer after the season, but it seemed like a mere formality and not an expression of enthusiasm.

The very day that Steve became a free agent, however, his old team, the Phoenix Suns, called his agent and made an incredible offer. Steve accepted. After six years in Dallas, when he went from a bench player who was booed by the home fans to an NBA superstar, Steve was on his way back to the team that drafted him in 1996 and made his dreams come true.

CHAPTER FIVE

RETURN OF THE PHOENIX

"I definitely won this award because of my role on the team."

Steve, after being named MVP

Steve was an intensely loyal player. That's why he wanted to stay in Dallas so much, and that's also why he was willing to return to Phoenix, where his career began. After the 2003-04 season, Dallas signed Dirk and Michael to long-term contracts but the team didn't try to do the same for Steve. This was very hurtful because he believed that he had been as important as his two friends in building the Mavericks into one of the best teams in the NBA.

The Suns, on the other hand, rolled out the red carpet for Steve. The team had two young superstars named Amare Stoudemire and Shawn Marion, but it was one of the worst teams in the league with a woeful record that year of just 29-53. Steve wanted to win a championship as much as any player, so he could have waited for the top teams to make him an offer. But he felt like the Suns really wanted him to play in Phoenix, and the team was offering about double the money Dallas had offered. "It was so clear they wanted me more than Dallas," Steve said after signing with Phoenix. "It was an absolute no-brainer."

> "It was so clear they wanted me more than Dallas," Steve said after signing with Phoenix.

Suns' general manager Bryan Colangelo was direct in his praise for Steve: "We know the impact that this player will have on us," he said at the press conference to re-introduce Steve to Phoenix. "I can't say enough about the character and leadership and the desire that Steve Nash will bring to this team."

Perhaps Steve also returned to Phoenix because he knew he could make this *his* team. The Suns won only 29 games in '03-'04, but with Steve leading an attack featuring Amare and Shawn, he knew the team could get much better very quickly.

The fall of 2004 was a hectic one for Steve. First, he and Alejandra had to move. Second, Steve had to get ready for a new team. And, third, he was about to become a father—twice! On October 14, 2004, Alejandra had twins – Lourdes and Isabella – a joy for the happy couple that now had two little lives to give their love to.

On the court, Steve had a career year and the Suns made one of the most incredible improvements in NBA history. Steve ran the offense, and it was decided by coach Mike D'Antoni that the tam would use its speed as its main weapon. So, when Steve took the ball up court, he could pass to Amare or Shawn or Quentin Richardson, another free agent who was a great shooter. Or, he could shoot himself. It seemed like the possibilities were unlimited or, at least, so many that their opponents wouldn't know what to do.

> *Steve had a career year and the Suns made one of the most incredible improvements in NBA history.*

Despite starting the year with seven of ten games on the road, the Suns roared out to a 12-2 record and didn't let up all season long. They averaged more than 110 points a game, the best average in ten years, and they finished with a record of 62-20. Their road record of 31-10 was one of the best of all time. During one stretch early in the year, the Suns won eleven games in a row and Steve set an NBA record with at least ten assists in all of those games. Steve missed seven games during the year with injuries, and in those games Phoenix won only twice. Not surprisingly given the skill of his teammates, Steve led the entire NBA in assists, averaging 11.5 per game. He shot better than 50 per cent from the field and had a career best in rebounds as well.

Perhaps Steve's best game, from a personal standpoint, came the night of March 30, 2005, against Philadelphia. He recorded a triple-double in that game, meaning he had double digits in points (12), assists (12), and rebounds (13). This is a rare feat in the NBA. More amazingly, he did this in just over half a game!

Steve goes along the outside and then drives hard to the net past Miami's Gary Payton who can offer only flimsy defence.

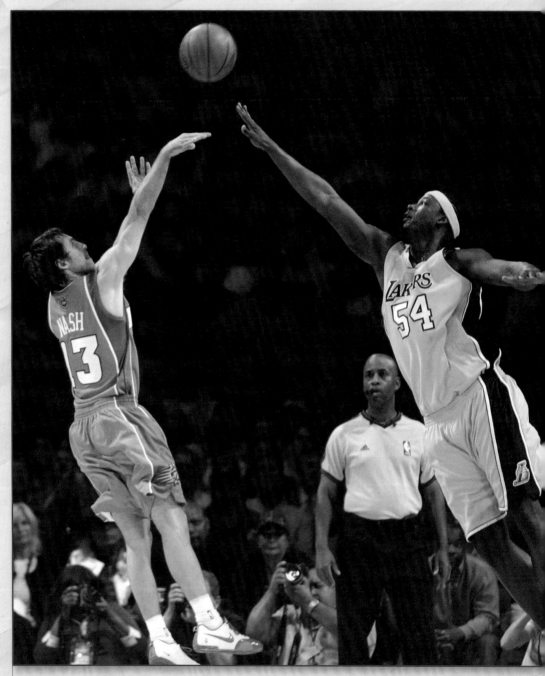

Steve's three-point attempt is almost blocked by the Lakers'
Kwame Brown during the 2007 playoffs.

Steve Nash: Most Valuable Player

As the season neared its end, everyone started talking about Steve being the MVP of the league. On May 8, 2005, the rumours were confirmed and he was, indeed, named the most valuable player in the entire league! Steve became only the third point guard ever to win the award, and his win was more amazing because of the players who were considered second best—Shaquille O'Neal, Kobe Bryant, Allen Iverson, to name just a few. Of course, he was also the first Canadian to win the NBA's player of the year award as well.

Steve won not because he was the tallest or the strongest or because he had the most amazing slam dunks. He didn't win because he was the flashiest or the richest or played in the best basketball city. He won because he was, quite simply, the most effective player, game in, game out. "I definitely won this award because of my role on the team," he said. "I didn't win this because I overpower people or I'm dominating people with physical ability, whether it's jumping ability or strength or height."

As the season neared its end, everyone started talking about Steve being the MVP of the league.

"Shaq" was humble in placing second in the voting: "It's been a good year for Steve. He had twins...He's playing great basketball. Congratulations, Steve. Congratulations to the Canadian people. It's a great honour."

While the personal honour was wonderful, Steve was thinking about an NBA championship as well. The Suns easily eliminated Memphis in the first round of the playoffs, sweeping them aside in four routine games. That set the stage for a best-of-seven date against the Dallas Mavericks, the team that had let Steve go at the start of the season. It was a series that defined his MVP season.

Game one was all Phoenix, but Dallas eked out a win in game two to even the series. Steve scored 27 points and added an amazing 17 assists in the third game to lead the Suns to victory, but that was only the beginning. In the fourth game, Steve scored a career high 48 points, but Dallas somehow managed to win and even the series again. Steve would not be denied.

In game five, he recorded a rare playoff triple-double, hitting for 34 points and adding 13 rebounds and 12 assists. "Nash played like an MVP tonight," Dallas coach Avery Johnson conceded afterward. "We had no answers for him. We tried everything humanly possible...He was a monster in the second half."

> *"We tried everything humanly possible.... He was a monster in the second half."*

Game six was more Steve Nash MVP material. Dallas led the game by 16 points halfway through the third quarter, but he simply stepped up his game at the perfect time. In the last minute of the game, Steve scored an amazing eight points including a three-pointer with five seconds left to send the game into overtime. In the extra quarter, he scored seven more points and added two assists and took the Suns to the conference finals. He ended with 39 points, 12 assists, and nine rebounds. He made his last five shots in a row under the most pressure of situations.

"He made some unbelievable plays, not only today to win the game, but in every game they won," friend and opponent Dirk Nowitzki said afterward. "I've never seen him play better than this. I think he really wanted to show all of Dallas what we missed."

Unfortunately, Steve and the Suns simply ran out of miracles. Steve set another record by becoming the first player ever to score at least 25 points and ten rebounds in four successive playoff games. The Suns were eliminated in five

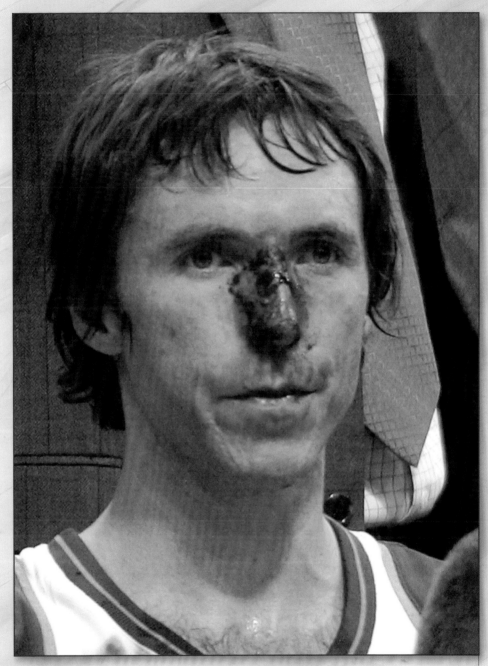

The picture of dejection, Steve sits on the sidelines with a banged-up nose during the dying moments of the team's last-minute loss to San Antonio in game one of their 2007 playoff series.

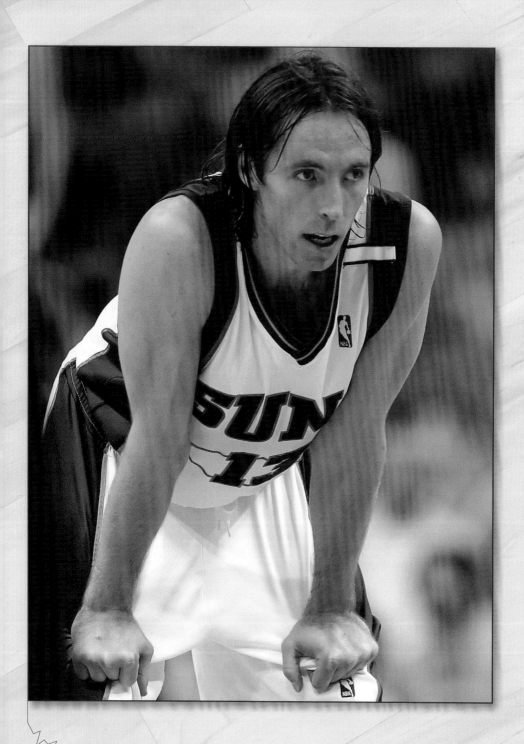

Steve makes another great left-handed lay-up against the Lakers' Kwame Brown during game two of the Phoenix-Los Angeles series in the 2006 playoffs.

Always focused, always ready to play, Steve is the poster boy for concentration.

Steve hugs Tim Duncan of San Antonio after game six of the teams' playoff series in 2007.

Steve Nash: Most Valuable Player

games in the conference finals, but a team that had gone from 29 wins to one that had 62 in the regular season and advanced to the third round of the playoffs was one that had made enormous improvement.

The year got better for Steve in all ways when he married Alejandra a few months later. He was also named winner of the Lou Marsh Trophy as Canada's top athlete for the year.

The 2005-06 season was another extraordinary one for Steve and proved once and for all that he was the best player in the game. During the off season, the Suns lost some of their best players to free agency and injury, leaving Steve to guide a virtually new team. Yet by the end of the season, he and the Suns had almost as sensational a season as they had the previous year. Quentin Richardson was traded, as was shooting guard Joe Johnson, and Amare Stoudemire missed virtually the entire year with two knee injuries.

> *The year got better for Steve in all ways when he married Alejandra.*

Steve, though, was magical. He once again led the league in assists (averaging 10.5 per game) as well as free-throw percentage (better than 92 per cent). He increased his scoring to nearly 19 points a night and his field-goal average was a career best 51.2 per cent. He also made the First All-Star Team again and was voted a starter to the All-Star Game. In all, the Suns finished with a 54-28 record, and for the fifth year in a row, a team led by Steve led the league in scoring (the last two with Phoenix, the previous three before that with Dallas). That alone proved his value to any team he played on.

On May 7, 2006, Steve was voted the NBA's most valuable player—again. It was an historic announcement. Only eight players in the history of the NBA had ever won the honour twice in a row, and for a skinny Canadian with a mop of hair to be a part of that elite group was, well, amazing. The award was also a way of paying tribute to his contributions to his team. While other players like LeBron James may be more skilled individually, what no one doubted for a moment was that Steve made every player around him a better player. He didn't just star on his own—he made everyone a star!

"I have to admit it's a little bit uncomfortable to be singled out amongst all these great players two years in a row," he said of the honour. "I have to pinch myself. I can't believe I'm standing here today. I couldn't believe it last year. But, I'm not going to give it back."

> For a skinny Canadian with a mop of hair to be a part of that elite group was, well, amazing.

Steve still had work to do, though. The Suns were set to play the Los Angeles Lakers in the opening round of the playoffs, a team led by Kobe Bryant who only a short time ago had scored an unbelievable 81 points in a single game against the Toronto Raptors. The series went very badly for Phoenix almost from the beginning. Although the Suns won the first game, they lost the next three in a row, and the Lakers seemed poised to cruise to a quick series win. Worse still, Steve was playing poorly, making wrong decisions and bad giveaways, and just not playing his usual brilliant game. Only seven times in NBA history had a team rallied from 3-1 down in a series to win, so Steve had to make amends quickly. Guess what? He did.

In game five, Steve had 22 points in a solid 114-97 win. In game six, he had 32 points and 13 assists in a 126-118 overtime win. And, in game seven, the Suns pulled away with an easy 121-90 win, the first time since 1970 that a team had rallied from three losses in a row to win. That gave the Suns a playoff date against the other L.A. team, the Clippers, and although it lacked the same drama, it also went to a seventh game.

Steve holds his MVP trophy high in the air for the home fans prior to a playoff game in 2005. He was the first Canadian to win the prestigious honour.

Needless to say, Steve was the best player on the court in that decisive game. He scored 29 points and added eleven assists, and the Suns rolled to an easy 127-107 victory to advance to the conference finals again. They were going to play Steve's old team again, the Dallas Mavericks.

There were striking parallels between Steve's career and Wayne Gretzky's. Wayne played many years with the Edmonton Oilers before being traded to the Los Angeles Kings. In his first year with the Kings, he eliminated his old team in the playoffs, but the year after the Oilers eliminated the Kings. In Steve's case, his new team, Phoenix, eliminated his old team, Dallas, the previous year, and now Dallas eliminated the Suns.

> **Steve was the best player on the court in that decisive game.**

Phoenix won the first game thanks to Steve's 27-point performance, but Dallas won the next three to take control of the series. Phoenix won game five, but game six was all Dallas. Steve's old friend, Dirk Nowitzki, was on his way to the NBA finals, and Steve had to fly home disappointed. He was league MVP for a second time, but he still didn't have his championship title.

The 2006-07 season started with another honour for Steve as Santa Clara invited him back to retire his number 11 jersey. He then led the Suns to another great season and another berth in the playoffs. Their regular season record of 61-21 was second only to Dallas, and as a result they played the Lakers in the first round of the playoffs again. But, the series didn't have the intensity of the previous year—Phoenix was just too good. The Suns won the best-of-seven in five games, but game four stands out because of Steve's amazing 23 assists, a personal best and one shy of the NBA record.

Steve holds his twin daughters Lourdes (foreground) and Isabella in the summer of 2006 prior to his charity basketball game in Vancouver.

In the second round, the Suns played the San Antonio Spurs, a team led by Tim Duncan and Tony Parker. Although Steve tried to make it close, the Spurs won in six games. The highlight of this series came toward the end of the first game when Steve collided with Tony. Steve suffered a bad cut to his nose and had to leave the game with less than a minute to go and his team trialing by just two points. With Steve off the court, the Spurs won the game and went on to win the series. He might be the best basketball player in the world, but Steve was realizing how difficult it was to win an NBA championship.

PLAYING FOR CANADA

CHAPTER SIX

"The Canadian National
Team is part of Steve
Nash's success story"

Leo Rautins

Steve's first taste of wearing the maple leaf was a brief one. Back in the summer of 1991, he had a tryout with the national junior team before being the final cut. After a superb Grade 12 season, and then a remarkable first year at Santa Clara, he made the national junior team with ease in the summer of 1993. Although the team narrowly failed to qualify for the world championship, Steve then went on to play for Canada at the World University Games in Buffalo later that summer. He led Canada to the finals against a mighty team from the United States, and although Canada lost, 95-90, Steve had made another amazing impression. He had eleven points and 17 assists in that game, and it was clear he was a star in the making.

Steve realized that Basketball Canada represented a great opportunity for him. For one, he got to play for his country, something that every athlete wants to do during his career. Second, by playing at a world-class level, he was able improve every aspect of his game. Third, as the star player almost from day one, Steve was able to develop leadership skills which he could bring back to his university or NBA team. Every chance Steve could play for Canada, he did.

> *Steve then went on to play for Canada at the World University Games.*

His next opportunity came the very next summer at the World Championships. They were held that year in Toronto, and Steve led the team to a 7th-place finish. It was his first chance to play at the senior level in international play, and again as the challenge got tougher, Steve rose to the occasion.

Always looking to improve his game, Steve played for Canada again in the summer of 1997 after his first year in the NBA, helping Canada qualify in a regional tournament for the 1998 World Championships.

Steve faced an even greater challenge in the summer of 1999 as he tried to help Canada qualify for the 2000 Olympics. There were only two teams that would come out of the regional tournaments from North, Central, and South America, and everyone knew that the USA, with a team of all NBA superstars, had pretty much locked up one place. That meant that Canada would be one of nine countries competing for the other spot.

The summer qualifying was dubbed "Mission Impossible" by Team Canada, but with Steve Nash that which is impossible suddenly becomes possible when he's playing. Indeed, Canada rolled through the games, winning one after another, until a decisive confrontation against Puerto Rico on its home court. Steve put on a clinic, as they say. He scored 26 points before a nasty crowd, leading Canada to an 83-71 win and a trip to the finals against the USA. The win meant Canada, incredibly, had qualified for the 2000 Olympics in Sydney, Australia. Steve was named MVP of this qualification tournament even though Canada lost a close game in the finals.

> *Steve was named captain of the team, and he performed with a hero's sense of greatness.*

His greatest contribution to his country, though, came in 2000 at the Summer Olympics. Steve had been asked by Great Britain to represent that country (because his parents were British, he also held a passport from that country), but he declined and opted to play for Canada. It was the first time Canada had been to the Olympics in basketball since 1988.

Steve was named captain of the team, and he performed with a hero's sense of greatness. In the first game, Canada posted a significant upset by beating the host nation convincingly, 101-90. Canada then followed up with wins over Angola, 99-54, and Spain, 91-77, before losing to the powerful Russians, 77-59. In its last game of the round robin, Canada faced Yugoslavia, the

Steve scores two points against Puerto Rico on August 21, 2003, during Canada's 89-79 win at the Olympic qualifying tournament.

Steve squeezes past Brazilian guard Valter Da Silva on August 26, 2003. during the Olympic qualifying tournament.

world champions in 1998 and the silver medalists from the 1996 Olympics in Atlanta, Georgia. The last time the teams played, at the 1998 World Championships, Yugoslavia won by 45 points.

This only motivated Steve all the more. He played perhaps the most inspired game of his life, scoring 26 points, making eight assists, and collecting another eight rebounds. More important, in the final minutes with the game on the line, Steve was nearly perfect, nailing three-point shots and hitting all ten free throws with a grace under pressure only the greats are capable of.

Some 14 of his points came in those final minutes, and he was three-for-three for three-pointers in that stretch as well. It was a clutch effort that awed even his teammates. "That was all guts," Rowan Barrett said of Steve's play. "Outside of all the skill he possesses, he's got a heart, a heart you rarely see in sports," he went on. The 83-75 win shocked the basketball world and made Canada a legitimate medal contender now as Canada finished first in the Group B standings.

> "We could have been in the championship game. We were good enough."

Canada then faced France, the fourth-place team in Group A, in a crossover quarter-finals match, but this time it was the French who pulled off a surprise win, eliminating Canada, 68-63. Steve left the court in tears, knowing a great chance had been heart-breakingly lost. France went on to the gold-medal game, and Canada beat Russia 86-83 in double overtime to finish in seventh position.

"I felt like I let everyone down," Steve said right after the loss to France. "We could have been in the championship game. We were good enough...Hopefully, we created some positive energy and momentum. Hopefully, kids [in Canada] will be inspired to play. That's what I really hope."

Said Leo Rautins of Steve's time with the national team over the years: "I don't think he would be where he is without the national team. Back in the early days of his pro career, when he was struggling in the NBA, people would still see him putting together killer performances for Canada. That makes people more willing to believe in you, to stick with you. The Canadian National Team is part of Steve Nash's success story."

Steve's most recent games in a Canadian jersey came in 2003 in the qualifying tournament for the 2004 Olympics. Everything about that summer was different from 1999, though. Steve was now the only NBA player on the team, so opponents merely focused their defence on Steve and knew they could win. Canada finished a disappointing fourth and failed to qualify for Athens, but Steve was named MVP again for another outstanding effort.

> *The drive to be the best, to prove himself over and over again, has always motivated Steve more than money or fame.*

At that time, he said he had likely played his last games for Canada, but you never know. The drive to be the best, to prove himself over and over again, has always motivated Steve more than money or fame. As long as his body is willing, his heart will certainly tell him to play for his country, for there is no greater way to put your talents to use than for the glory of your home.

Steve Nash is a great NBA star and a tribute to all that is good about basketball, but he is also the greatest basketball player Canada has ever produced. Wayne Gretzky may have been his idol as a kid, but Steve is now the hero to thousands of kids across the world for the way he plays the game—all heart.

After defeating China 94-66 in an exhibition game in Vancouver in 2002, Canada's Steve Nash tosses mini basketballs into the crowd.

Steve draws two Charlotte defenders to him, Melvin Ely (left) and Kareem Rush, allowing him to get a man free for the pass.

Steve Nash: Most Valuable Player

STEVE NASH: BY THE NUMBERS

Steven John Nash

6'3" 195 lbs.

b. Johannesburg, South Africa, February 7, 1974

NBA Statistics

Regular Season

Year	Team	GP	MPG	FG	3P%	FT%	APG	PPG
1996-97	PHO	65	10.5	.423	.418	.824	2.1	3.3
1997-98	PHO	76	21.9	.459	.415	.860	3.4	9.1
1998-99	DAL	40	31.7	.363	.374	.826	5.5	7.9
1999-2000	DAL	56	27.4	.477	.403	.882	4.9	8.6
2000-01	DAL	70	34.1	.487	.406	.895	7.3	15.6
2001-02	DAL	82	34.6	.483	.455	.887	7.7	17.9
2002-03	DAL	82	33.1	.465	.413	.909	7.3	17.7
2003-04	DAL	78	33.5	.470	.405	.916	8.8	14.5
2004-05	PHO	75	34.3	.502	.431	.887	11.5	15.5
2005-06	PHO	79	35.4	.512	.439	.921	10.5	18.8
2006-07	PHO	76	35.3	.532	.455	.899	11.6	18.6
Totals		779	30.5	.483	.426	.896	7.6	14.0

Playoffs

Year	Team	GP	MPG	FG	3P%	FT%	APG	PPG
1996-97	PHO	4	3.8	.222	.250	.000	0.3	1.3
1997-98	PHO	4	12.8	.444	.200	.625	1.8	5.5
2000-01	DAL	10	37.0	.417	.410	.882	6.4	13.6
2001-02	DAL	8	40.4	.432	.444	.971	8.8	19.5
2002-03	DAL	20	36.5	.447	.487	.873	7.3	16.1
2003-04	DAL	5	39.4	.386	.375	.889	9.0	13.6
2004-05	PHO	15	40.7	.520	.389	.919	11.3	23.9
2005-06	PHO	20	39.9	.502	.368	.912	10.2	20.4
2006-07	PHO	11	37.5	.463	.487	.891	13.3	18.9
Totals		97	36.1	.468	.419	.899	8.8	17.3

Index: PHO=Phoenix Suns; DAL=Dallas Mavericks; GP=games played; MPG=minutes per game/average; FG=field goal shooting percentage; 3P%=three-point shooting percentage; APG=assists per game/average; PPG=points per game/average

GLOSSARY

assist—make a pass to a player who scores a basket

backboard—the area directly behind the net

basket—the rim and mesh into which the ball must be shot to score

beyond the arc—the area outside the three-point line, which is shaped like an arc

blocked shot—deflecting the ball away from an opponent who is in the act of shooting

bucket—slang for basket

deuce—slang for two points (i.e., a basket)

dish (off)—slang for pass

drive (to the net)—manoeuvre with force to the basket

dunk—put the ball in the basket by jumping to the net and putting the ball directly in the net

fade away jumper—jump shot whereby the player's body recedes from the basket during the shooting motion

foul—illegal physical contact with an opponent

free throw—shot from the free-throw line made as a result of a foul

glass—slang for backboard

go to the line—take a free throw

goaltending—act of slapping the ball away form the basket while it is on its downward course to the net itself

hardcourt—slang for court

jump ball—"faceoff" in which two players try to retrieve the ball tossed in the air by an official

jumper—slang for jump shot

man-on-man defence—defensive strategy in which every player guards an opponent

nail—score (i.e., he nailed a three-pointer with one second left in the game)

offensive foul—foul committed by a member of the team in possession of the ball

quarter—one of four periods of play, 12 minutes long in the NBA

rebound—loose ball after a missed shot

roundball—slang for basketball

shot clock—clock which allows a team 24 seconds to make a shot

steal—strip an opponent of the ball

technical foul—foul for unsportsmanlike conduct

three pointer—shot which gives a team three points

throw down—score (i.e., he threw down 24 points in the game)

turnover—allow an opponent to strip the ball off a player

zone defence—defensive strategy in which players guard a particular area of their own end

Steve executes a routine jump shot, something of a rarity in the NBA, with time to spare and no one in his face.

Acknowledgements

The author would like to thank the few people who have contributed to the book directly or indirectly. First and foremost, to publisher Jordan Fenn for his ongoing support of this book series. Also to the design team of Michael Gray and Rob Scanlan at First Image for their expert work. To agent Dean Cooke for faithful support of the various projects he has helped steer along. And to family, notably to my wife, Emma Grace, for her constant smile through the long hours and hectic schedule. Without all of the above, this book couldn't have happened. Cheers.